AMAZING ANIMALS

CHIPMUNKS

BY MARI BOLTE

CREATIVE EDUCATION • CREATIVE PAPERBACKS

Published by Creative Education
and Creative Paperbacks
P.O. Box 227, Mankato, Minnesota 56002
Creative Education and Creative Paperbacks
are imprints of The Creative Company
www.thecreativecompany.us

Design by The Design Lab
Production by Blue Design
Art direction by Graham Morgan

Images by flickr/Biodiversity Heritage Library, 8, 23; Getty Images/Ed Reschke, 14; Pexels/Adriaan Greyling, 5, Chris F, 20, NAUSHIL | SKYHAWK. ASIA, 9; Unsplash/Jessica Eirich, cover, 1; Wikimedia Commons/Cephas, 6, 21, Davidlamma, 13, ForestWander, 17, Frank Schulenburg / CC BY-SA 4.0, 18, J Doll, 16, Phil Armitage, 7, Rhododendrites, 2, Vickie J Anderson, 10

Library of Congress Cataloging-in-Publication Data
Names: Bolte, Mari author
Title: Chipmunks / by Mari Bolte.
Description: Mankato, Minnesota : Creative Education and Creative Paperbacks, [2026] | Series: Amazing animals | Includes bibliographical references and index. | Audience: Ages 6-9 | Audience: Grades 2-3 | Summary: "Explore the charming world of chipmunks with this delightful zoology title for elementary-aged readers. Discover chipmunks' habitats, behaviors, and unique traits, and enjoy a captivating tale about how chipmunks got their stripes"— Provided by publisher.
Identifiers: LCCN 2025011360 (print) | LCCN 2025011361 (ebook) | ISBN 9798895810538 library binding | ISBN 9798896800064 paperback | ISBN 9798895811795
ebook Subjects: LCSH: Chipmunks—Juvenile literature
Classification: LCC QL737.R68 B65 2026 (print) | LCC QL737.R68 (ebook) | DDC 599.36/4—dc23/eng/20250612
LC record available at https://lccn.loc.gov/2025011360
LC ebook record available at https://lccn.loc.gov/2025011361

Printed in China

Table of Contents

Chipmunks are also called ground squirrels. However, not all ground squirrels are chipmunks.

Chipmunks are small, striped **rodents** with big eyes and ears. They are part of the squirrel family. Chipmunks live in forests and plains. They also live in mountains, deserts, and even towns and cities.

rodent a small mammal with teeth that never stop growing

Eastern chipmunks are the largest species. Least chipmunks are the smallest.

There are 25 different **species** of chipmunk. All but one live in North America. The eastern chipmunk and least chipmunk are the most common. Chipmunks hop and bound along the ground. They can also climb trees.

species a group of animals with similar characteristics

Chipmunks are usually reddish-brown, brown, or gray, with white tummies. They have darker stripes along their backs, with white or cream lines mixed in. In winter, their fur is thicker and duller. In spring and summer, it is brighter.

Chipmunks have two tan and five dark brown stripes on their bodies.

Chipmunks are small. From nose to tail, they are between 5.5 and 12 inches (14–30.5 centimeters) long. Their tails are used for balance. When chipmunks run, their tails stick straight up in the air.

Chipmunks have four toes on their front paws and five on their back.

A chipmunk's diet includes both bugs and plants. Chipmunks even eat meat if they can find it. Nuts, fruit, and mushrooms are easy to find. Chipmunks might steal from bird feeders and pet food bowls, too!

Some chipmunks are hunters. They look for small snakes and bird eggs.

Chipmunk burrows can be 10 feet (3 meters) or longer. There are usually several rooms for storage, sleeping, and giving birth.

Some chipmunks dig underground burrows. They make them close to big **structures**, such as houses or trees. There are always more ways in and out. Other chipmunks build nests in logs, trees, or bushes. A few even make their way into attics!

structure a building or object made up of many different assembled parts

Chipmunks in places with a long summer may have two litters per year.

Chipmunks usually live alone, except during mating season. **Gestation** lasts for about a month. They usually have two to eight babies called kits or pups. Six weeks later, the young chipmunks are ready to leave the burrow. Two weeks after that, they are on their own.

gestation the length of an animal's pregnancy

Some animals look for chipmunk caches to steal from in the winter.

In the winter,

chipmunks take a long nap called **torpor**. Their body temperature drops. They do not eat or drink. Unlike **hibernating** animals, chipmunks do not store fat. Instead, they spend months collecting piles of food called caches. They wake up every few days, have a snack, and then go back to sleep.

torpor a state of physical or mental inactivity

hibernate pass the winter in a resting state

Cheek pouches help chipmunks carry food back to their cache. Carrying food this way also frees up the chipmunk's front legs in case it needs to get away quickly. The pouches can stretch three times larger than the chipmunk's head!

The eastern chipmunk can hold up to 70 sunflower seeds in its cheek pouches.

A Chipmunk Tale

The Haudenosaunee people of northeast North America have a tale about how the chipmunk got its stripes. Bear was showing off his strength. Chipmunk challenged him to stop the sun from rising. Bear tried and tried but couldn't do it. Chipmunk laughed at him. Angry, Bear caught Chipmunk and held him down with his paw. Chipmunk squirmed and struggled. As he wriggled free, the tips of Bear's claws scraped Chipmunk's back, leaving three stripes.

Read More

Austen, Lily. *Chipmunk or Squirrel?* Minneapolis: Jump!, Inc., 2025.

Chang, Kirsten. *Baby Chipmunk or Baby Skunk?* Minneapolis: Bellwether Media, Inc., 2025.

Herschbach, Elisabeth. *Rodents Infest.* Mendota Heights, Minn.: Apex Editions, 2025.

Websites

Britannica Kids: Chipmunk
https://kids.britannica.com/kids/article/chipmunk/352953
Learn some cool facts about chipmunks.

National Geographic Kids: Chipmunk
https://kids.nationalgeographic.com/animals/mammals/facts/chipmunk
Fun facts about these adorable animals.

Note: Every effort has been made to ensure that the websites listed above are suitable for children, that they have educational value, and that they contain no inappropriate material. However, because of the nature of the Internet, it is impossible to guarantee that these sites will remain active indefinitely or that their contents will not be altered.

Index